EARTH *at* PERIHELION

EARTH at PERIHELION

Pamela Hobart Carter

MoonPath Press

Copyright © 2025 Pamela Hobart Carter
All rights reserved.

No part of this publication may be reproduced, distributed, or transmitted in any form or by any means whatsoever without written permission from the publisher, except in the case of brief excerpts for critical reviews and articles. All inquiries should be addressed to MoonPath Press.

Poetry
ISBN 979-8-9899487-8-9

Cover Photo: Pamela Hobart Carter

Author photo: Omar Willey

Book design by Tonya Namura,
using Garamond Premier Pro

MoonPath Press, an imprint of Concrete Wolf Poetry Series, is dedicated to publishing the finest poets living in the U.S. Pacific Northwest.

MoonPath Press
c/o Concrete Wolf
PO Box 2220
Newport, OR 97365-0163

MoonPathPress@gmail.com

http://MoonPathPress.com

For Aunt Bee.

ACKNOWLEDGMENTS

Thank you to the publishers and editors of these enterprises in which these poems have appeared, some in slightly altered form:

Bengaluru Review: "Sisters in December"

BlueHouse Journal: "Ocean Tastes"

Burningword Literary Journal: "Succession"

Flapper Press Poetry Café: "Only Fools"

Flight of the Dragonfly: "Life Meeting Life" and "Reverberations"

Her Imaginary Museum (Kelsay Books, 2020): "Starry Nights"

Heron Tree: "Latitudes"

I Sing the Salmon Home: Poems from Washington State edited by Rena Priest (Empty Bowl Press, 2023): "*Suquamish Waters*"

Last Stanza: "*Morse* Is Walrus Is Home"

Midway Journal: "Cyclone Approach"

Neologism: "Solstice Crow"

Only Connect (Yavanika Press, 2024): "When We Meet in the Future" and "'Even Birds Came Down'"

The Orchards Poetry Journal: "Red Right Returning"

Orenaug Mountain: "Take My Hand...My Whole Life"

Parks & Points & Poems: "Hiking to Red Mountain Pass" and "About the Rivers"

Pidgeonholes: "From the Point of View of the Hurricane"

Poetry in Public: "Trailhead Direct"

Poets for Science: "At the Center of Your Eye Is a Blackhole"

Pontoon: "Her Historical Geology" and "Latitudes"

Proem: "What the Viewer Sees"

Random Sample: "She Would Say She Swam with Her Brother"

The Seattle Star: "Bridged," "Not a Fairy Tale," "One Certain Thing," "Perihelion Pantoum," "Surface Evidence," "When…After…In," and "Yearning"

Sky Island Journal: "A Shape of Time"

Washington Poetic Routes: "Know the Duwamish Waterway"

What Rough Beast/Indolent Books: "Sown"

NonBinary Review/Zoetic Press: "We Return to the Vastness"

Thank you to the inspiring, encouraging, and helpful friends and family who write with me, listen to first drafts, mark up my margins, listen to further drafts, and articulate their wisdom.

David Mills said the words that inspired "*From the Point of View of the Star*," and Robert M. L. Raynard took the photographs that inspired "Bridged," "'Even Birds Came Down,'" and "On My Couch I Am."

And to Milton for "subtle thief" in "A Shape of Time."

TABLE OF CONTENTS

Acknowledgments   vii

I HER HISTORICAL GEOLOGY

Her Historical Geology   5
We Return to the Vastness   7
French Scenes   8
A Shape of Time   9
A Solidity of Space   10
Ocean Tastes   12
Cyclone Approach   13
From the Point of View of the Hurricane   15
She Would Say She Swam with Her Brother   16
Palisades   18
Will I Die on This Wednesday Hike?   20
Weakness   21
Start Here   22
Hiking to Red Mountain Pass   23
About the Rivers   24

II EARTH AT PERIHELION

Perihelion Pantoum   27
At the Center of Your Eye Is a Black Hole   28
The Curve   29
Red Right Returning   30
From the Point of View of the Star,   31
Signals, Dreams   32
Trailhead Direct   34
Starry Nights   35
Take My Hand…My Whole Life   36
Letter to My Daughter   37
Succession   38

Sisters in December	39
Yearning	41
Thousands of Eyes	42
Reverberations	43
Solstice Crow	44
Of One Mind	45
Suquamish Waters	46
Smoothie	47
When We Meet in the Future	49
What the Viewer Understands	51

III RIGHT PLANET

Not a Fairy Tale	55
Morse Is Walrus Is Home	56
Life Meeting Life	58
Knots	60
Sown	62
Latitudes	63
Know the Duwamish Waterway	64
Surface Evidence	66
"Even Birds Came Down"	67
Only Fools	68
Bridged	69
We Do Not Always Need the Map	70
On My Couch I Am	72
Not Knowing/Knowing	73
When…After…In	75
His Odyssey	76
Suppose It Is Here	77
Tunnel Solo	78
One Certain Thing	80
About the Author	81

EARTH at PERIHELION

I
HER HISTORICAL GEOLOGY

HER HISTORICAL GEOLOGY

For a decade she led the geology department at a
    prestigious liberal arts school
in the suburbs of a northeastern American city. In the
    rusting Chevy van,

all the college could afford, she drove handfuls of students
    along winding roads
into ancient rounded mountains to study exposures
    dynamited

as if expressly for her lectures—she patting rock walls,
    inviting protégés to smack hammers
against schist for chunks to hold to louped eyes to find each
    mineral she catalogued,

especially the garnets because they were her favorite for
    their crimson translucence
and diamond-shaped facets and for how they reminded her
    of the wonder of crystal faces

always telling the minuscule molecular structure in their
    perfect larger geometries
since that is how matter clings to matter, in lattices and
    sheets and at particular angles

fixed by the tiniest particles zipping around at the fastest
    speeds
in the smallest orbits. She was a different she in those days,
    allowed to be quieter,

before publishing the tract that told morning runners how to
    see the history of the landscapes
through which they trailed by touch of foot and heave of chest—

the lift of ground, the cut of wave, the fall of silt, and so to
    grok
roundnesses of bays, reposes of composite volcanos'
    gently sloped snow-clad cones,

localness of castle rampart stones, also sheer cliff-ness of
    divorce, fluvial aspects
of love, and corundum strength of mothers in labor, also
    their own corundum labors,

and their own fluvial aspects, and their own sheernesses,
    and their own localnesses
and reposes and roundnesses before their own extinctions.
    Her life in recent years

is, and resembles most, clogging clays sinking through cold
    meltwater to muddy bottoms
of glacial tarns of faraway frosty U-shaped valleys. Her
    death will go

as unremarked as a single spruce or orca or gabbro—yet
    your thorax
will fissure, your throat erode, your photos and mementos
    wash to sea

from tears overspilling levees banked around your fissile
    heart tissue
—and will leave no record.

WE RETURN TO THE VASTNESS

where we feel ourselves invisible
as pinpricks, as flicked cigarette ash
cold on landing on the sere expanse,
pinion pines unlit by our presence,
the stone floor unmoved, winds unimpressed.

From end to end of every vista
the rocks last as bands, once Saharas,
shallow salty reaches of sponge-filled seas,
estuaries carving channels through muddy banks,
deeper oceans where swam trilobites, land tracked
by creatures we've never met—and cannot—
blankets of hellred lava.

We return to visit ancient time,
to descend, to travel back and back
and back to a planet hotter,
to an Arizona underwater, on the margin
of one continent, another, farther, to depths
internal and before living cells,
to these ages of our nonexistence.

We return to marvel at this fleet stage—
our breathing, aware how recent our arrival,
how fast will come the departure,
how rare the event of us, grand and literate,
fatuous, feeble, animal, fatal, trivial.

FRENCH SCENES

*French playwrights begin a new scene
with each character entrance or exit.*

Tefnut, goddess of moisture, first launches your ancestry
on a fertile patch of soil, where the Nile floods annually
so teaching your thousandth great-grandparents
to craft not fortresses but thrifty wooden shacks,
simple to reframe.

    Fast-forward a couple of millennia to your
    first scene: you arrive on a fine spring evening,
    fourth child.

        In your second scene a grandfather
        departs the earth: you are fourteen.

            Next: scenes undergo large and
            rapid changes as remaining
            grandparents bid farewell.

                In a further flurry:
                your parents.

                    Then scenes flit by
                    at speed as you
                    bury friends who
                    headed backstage
                    for what you
                    believed were
                    quick costume
                    changes.

A SHAPE OF TIME

Time will tell truths of how we came to be,
how long atoms of us take to transform
into salt seas, salt seas into Lot's wife.

When we weep in solitude, tears sliding
into tissues and tossed in the trash can,
it is a waste. What if we assemble

on the sediment of the nearest shore
and sob, later today or tomorrow,
as time allows, and let sorrows, seaward,

run together? Time, we name *subtle thief*,
and fault with casting finite limits. But
we constructed ticking dials and Tuesdays.

Construe existence as sky, spread about
and over and around, and light and dark
on different lands below; reality

cut like a torus, a disk, a spun top,
a star map of a belted Greek hunter,
a tentacled spiraling galaxy,

a memory of post-blizzard snow forts,
a breeze lifting feathers of the resting
Western tanager by this bright water.

A SOLIDITY OF SPACE

                        In a dream I keep playing

        there is so much solidity
                that a father gets photographed
by the chance of his presence in my mind

      appearing   himself
  in an image for me and my cousin

both our fathers enjoy chairs in some yard
        shade and fence protecting their books and drinks

                Waking
  what startles me

      is that he takes up any space
                    seeing as he is gone

a space occupied with fullness
              and a strong sense of life

    The same way my cousin
        in the faraway East Coast where she lives
           listens to my call and hears so clearly
              she enters my mind

      herself
                  sees our dads

On a trip to Iceland I stand on the margin

geologists call rift
                        a margin like knife-gashed skin
bleeding or scarred   At one rift site the rock is a sharp
wall with a twin ac   ross from it in brown basalt
I think of the geolo   gist's sigh ecstatic from her own
fulfillment   rift   lava ridge and tectonic plate
space understood   by her mind and
by her work

OCEAN TASTES

Like sorrow.

Like dreams, like
wet coldness.

Lush prospects
present to us when
we name food—
sour lemon drops,
briny chowders,
delicacies of madeleines—
flavors of the world
on paper crockery.

Is it possible
to taste ocean
five miles
from the shore?

CYCLONE APPROACH

Of ominous skies we say
        we're under a blanket

                        Rain we describe as if bathed
            in turmoil at the foot of a cataract

      Because the world is almost round
it wears a belt of humidity

      Sash
              might be more accurate

                    I wear a heart on my sleeve

Sometimes it is my own heart
                    Sometimes it is a badge

        Forecasts contradict each other
    so shepherds gather in their flocks   wait
      to see the color of the sunrise is not red

No one expects these torrents heard in the wrong locations
    a barn   a stairwell   a fluorescent interior

            when ordinarily we sleep

First light flies in under the black layer
      neon pink and yellow   the shade of pollen
        from stamens of magenta tulips

      Look north to see the mountain range
                                and
    visibility carries us two hundred miles
    into another country

In the belief we may again be safe
                              we step outside

FROM THE POINT OF VIEW OF
THE HURRICANE

                      lovelier than murder livelier
                 than torture mightiest loudest
            widest darkest I am all the
          plagues descending plagues
         descending in synchronicity
     Hell on your doorstep Hell at your
    windowsill Hell to remind you you cursed
   your castoffs and sludge but I stir your boil and
  trouble stir the soup adore your ingredients a crispy
bridge a lowing bovine an impoverished parish widest
loudest mightiest darkest worship at slaughter time I topple
hotheaded governments rain down mightier than pens ships
and kings nations collapse   islands flee loudest
 lowing widest dark rain   down collapse a
  hotheadedbovine on your   troubled   door
   step mighty ships   and   bridges descend
    in synchronicity cursed   in slaughter (flee)
     I am all the hot hell headed slaughter   collapse
      descending rain down mightier   plagues dark
       castoffs and all sludge worship stir trouble
        in lowing synchronicity collapse dark
         slaughter cursed synchronicity hot
          headed governments rain down
           mightier pens and ships and
           dark kings cursed nations
         collapse on impoverished
        doorsteps topple on lovelier
       islands worship hell in sync
     worship animpoverishedparish
   (worship) worship me!

SHE WOULD SAY SHE SWAM WITH HER BROTHER

She would say she swam
with her brother. He dove
into the crashing surf, dove
through the incoming wall and swam.

The ocean tossed
him around and he smiled.
From her beach post she waved and smiled.
The ocean tossed

and churned. She inched
like a bride down an aisle, halted
when the waves never halted
but lapped her feet, inched

to her ankles, calves—showered
her with cold, with salt. She loved
the freshness, loved
the pull of grains underfoot while above waves showered.

Opposite onslaughts. She laughed.
But how to enter?
How to enter?
Between swells, when the water laughed,

she slipped in, and the tow took
her and held
her below, held
her against the sand, took

her chances to breathe,
surrounded her with translucent green, bore

down on her, bore
on her an imagined end, would not let her breathe.

Against the bottom she pushed.
A trough passed.
A crest passed.
Through the water she pushed.

She marched
from the sea, mounted
a windswept dune, mounted
calm, marched

to the driest spot and dropped
onto safety, panted,
blinked off her typical tears, panted,
recovered, dropped

any thought of—waited
for her brother. He wended
his way up from noisy foam, wended
his way to quiet, where she waited.

Did they sit
together to watch
the breakers? Or did she watch
alone and sit

alone? He drove
them home, damp and wrapped
in their towels. She wrapped
away her death as he drove.

PALISADES

A trickle
dampens the cliff.
Waterfall in melt season.
Coralroot waves magenta
in understory shade.
Incense of duff.
Blue sky.

We climb through the legs of giants,
peaceful earth-eaters,
uninterested in golden-egg layers
or magic lyres.
Their faces turn upward.
We see only
their long brown and gray trousers,
their green jackets.

Their pace downslope
relates to angle of repose,
to erosion. Our pace
reveals facts about gradient.
In one steep stretch
we meet a staircase.
Each riser a log
hewn lengthwise.
The banister a single
skinny trunk,
sanded smooth.
The steps enormous.
Designed for taller folk.
My legs are short.

At the first ledge
I spot below a white ribbon

—the river—braiding
through gravel.

Another hour higher,
the snowy top of Rainier signals hello
over the green ridges opposite.
Hello! Hello! Mountain, hello!

A glint on the valley floor
is a car. A fleck
reflecting sun.
This planet circles a star
more than 94 million miles away.
An ancient flaming orb
of hydrogen and helium.
I suck in a big lungful
of wild air,
slug my electrolyte drink,
and tread the return path.

My husband meets all the spiders.
I walk behind.

WILL I DIE ON THIS WEDNESDAY HIKE?

In the middle of Fryingpan Creek (a torrent,
wrongly named), I freeze. Not *in* the icy drink,
but like a doe in headlights—one foot on one rock,
one foot on another, hiking poles poking into the gravel—
channel bed. Balanced. Barely. I am a statue.
A thinking statue. A blinking, balking statue. Will I slip,
trip, misstep? Will the current sweep me downstream?
Usher me to the underworld? Will my head knock
against a block of Ohanapecosh? (Or does this glacial melt
flood through Tatoosh granodiorite? I forget
while I study my mortality mid-river.) Will I die
on this Wednesday hike to Summerland?
Why does the log bridge span only half the deluge?
I don't move. Don't move. Don't move.
Maybe I can stay forever in the middle
of Fryingpan Creek? Has Search and Rescue
ever been called to snatch some stupid cluck
from the stream? I see the truth.
I must shift my weight.
Will my knee give, snap, tear? Will I die today
on my way to Summerland? I tell myself I must move. I do.
I teeter to the log bridge. Make solid turf on the far side
and we tramp to the narrow lane lined with scrub,
with brambles, with squat conifers, and this is when
we meet the bear. She is big. Round. Indifferent.
In the trail. Headed down. Toward. Again, I cross
Fryingpan Creek—not lickety-split—but
at a steady clip. Efficient.
I choose a smarter route with a bear at my back.

WEAKNESS

If you are a little creek
responding to gravity
to find slab pre-cracked
is sweet. You trickle in.
When you freeze,
your expanding ice
will squeeze against
your bounding walls,
tease grain away
from grain, release the sands
into your cold stream—
and you'll flow with freedom.

What follows?
Goats, deer, elk,
their predators,
then blown seeds
that saltate across
rock peaks...
affix, root, bud,
and grow green.

Everything makes its ease
on ancient paths of weakness.

START HERE

the invisible hero slays a monster
       on an unmapped island

the children dream their futures
       without instruction

ancillary characters weep
       about absence
          and
       antagonists swarm unchecked

       note how peasants work the soil
          of the foreground so as to feed humanity

the winged boy vanishes
       into a corner of aquamarine—
          with a bit of a splash

poets and painters depict the scenes repeatedly

time spills past the reader
       with the racing heart who rushes
       to arrive at the end point

       which could come at any moment

HIKING TO RED MOUNTAIN PASS

Late summer, almost fall, it's like I've found my childhood
tucked under these cedars—

    and I am ten and lazing on hot stone,
    watching ants.

For the first time in a long time I feel safe,
now I know the old granite wall always

    waits for my remembering, somewhere
    at my physical center,

available, with you on this hike, or even at my city desk
as I scrounge for perfection

    (click sites for research, recheck
    links and spelling

as if these secure a famous future where you hear me,
and everyone gathers to listen to my wisdom).

    The past is contained
    in our dark insides,

coded in chemicals which replace daily. Somehow
they flow the known channels.

    The way sentences store a truth
    even if unwritten.

All day, anywhere, we may dive back to then.
At the pass we gaze north and south.

    We see into spaces where
    time is slow to round mountains.

ABOUT THE RIVERS

                Beside us
rivers administer
        our sense of time
               through water's rush

        like blood's throb
through our internal channels
               where currents surge
        faster when we're children

               meander
        in our middle-ages

        run steady
through spells of constancy

        swell after storms

                 My sadness at last
     went
     when I tracked a stretch
        of the Middle Fork

silver
                splashing

       through duff and diorite
                sun on its surface

I go to rivers for their indifference

        Rivers to set my crafts afloat
        Rivers to carry me out and deep

II
EARTH AT PERIHELION

PERIHELION PANTOUM

Today Earth is at perihelion.
It's hard to believe
we're closest to the sun.
Air hangs damp.

It's hard to believe
when sky hums gray,
air hangs damp,
and doves refuse their dule.

When sky hums gray
I turn this direction to see live things
but doves refuse their dule
and perch in isolation around the corner.

I turn this direction to see live things,
glimpse only a stranger
from this perch in isolation.
Earth flies nearest its star.

I glimpse only a stranger
at a distance from me.
Earth flies nearest its star:
Earth is at perihelion.

AT THE CENTER OF YOUR EYE IS A BLACK HOLE

The center of your eye
and mine is an opening

that looks like a perfect round,
an aperture through to soul,

to a surface crowded
with sensors—we're sensitive,

sensory beings. You see
into me through my pupil.

The daystar cinches
it for our safety—

too much staring blinds.
At so many exact cores

lie blank spots we mistake
for emptiness.

THE CURVE

Even a story that marches a straight line
from *once upon* to *ever after* curves,
must curve with the globe's roundness—

any flat surface a figment of abstraction,
an approximation across a small acre.
To be clear, the narrative pauses

for a brief explication of a term,
a context, a crucial detail from a past
as yet untold—necessary crenulations.

Pedestrians slow their steps,
sailors let sails luff, and passengers
of flying carpets settle onto zephyrs

or local thermals. Their paths spiral.
Each single minute holds eternity.
Each character's life spools.

The moon sails past, its face vacant.
A placid circle. Its skull, bald.
Its brain, massive.

RED RIGHT RETURNING

Sometimes you float familiar seas, find the liquid oscillates
to a famous song. Sometimes you drift
as if to a minor ballad, its melody a strange path,
the composer hurriedly jotting open and closed ovals
across an architecture of horizontal lines, keeping pace
as you move, matching your comings-about, your jibes,
your doldrums—the composer, of course,
none other than yourself

who, very late, maybe, close to the final moments,
remembers how a craft holds a channel, steers between
the red nun and the green can, a mooring ahead—
inevitable specter of your journey's end—

and whatever you ink,
whatever you believe you know, falls,
inadequate and overwhelming in the same surge,
because you adore your child or your cat
or how a downpour pulses its low percussion
against your hull and you want

always to be able to want

never to come ashore

FROM THE POINT OF VIEW OF THE STAR,

he says, as if the ball of hot gas sees time
with a circumference of eyes,
the event passes in a flash.
But, from the point of view
of the rest of the universe—
outside the black hole—
a form of eternity,
before the old star
turns new again.

We've all heard of the dark pools—
tremendous sucking vortices
that even tug in light. It's not how I see it.

From Earth, I witness a death,
an emptiness where once pulsed
a bright pinprick. After what he told me,
I wait for a return. Any moment now.

Standing on this ground, the only pull
I sense magnetizes my body,
keeps me from floating into space
to join the moon in orbit.

How do I know what I'm looking at?
From my point of view, so little I watch
matches the models, I trust to proofs
for their elegance, although incomplete,

and train my gaze on the motion of dots
in the sky, uncertain who owns the story.

SIGNALS, DREAMS

If interior signals firing resemble kindled stars,
        then our thoughts may smolder,
may crisp, may drift as snowflake ash, may sit
        like an unswept coal burner awaiting
Cinderella, or erupt and spew lava bombs
        or quick-melt a glacier residing
on a mental slope to set off a gushing slurry
        of mixed hot mud and boulders
down the twisted streambed, across the valley
        (where tiny lilies flower
around this season) and onto a wider, flatter expanse
        known for its fertility and mercurial coloring
—gold in spring, summer-jade, ruby, and then
        its diamond-sparkly winters—to blanket
what once seemed reasonable with inventions
        of fancy such as clever, speaking spiders,
miniature humans with gossamer wings
        of luna-moth green, and rainbows
like actual bridges on which we travel from dreariness
        to satisfaction, and come again to an ease
with ourselves, which enables sleep when sleepy;
        energy when wakeful; silence when words
fall short—when silence is desired; kind cleverness
        when siblings disagree; hunger
for the seedy strawberries volunteering at the corner
        of the yard when they appear; readiness for reversals

of magnetic poles when declinations veer irrelevant,
  and we may determine to dig into the soil
on this end of the prismed arch maybe-possibly-
  could-be forever, according to every kind of counter
conceived since cave folk—the fingers, the shadow stick,
  the sun clock, the waterwheel, the abacus,
the painted candle, the sandglass, the pocket watch,
  Big Ben, the ounce of radium, the Timex,
the pendulum, and every kind of counter
  not yet dreamed up (because we believe our planet
will always, everlastingly birth dreamers).

TRAILHEAD DIRECT

High on the volcano
we munched crackers
and nuts and gazed about
at the green meadow's bowl—
a palm, cupped. Through the fingers
of that hand (holding us in safety)
a creek mumbled in its own language.
We sat among fat marmots,
below a sun that warmed everything.

STARRY NIGHTS

Begin with night sky above sodium-lamp city—
Ursa Major, Orion, Cassiopeia,
Mars, Venus, Moon. You have seen
what the artist saw.

Between these, stars and planets
of her own invention drip off her paintbrush—
she loves the edge of science that touches chance,
and the painting was never to be a chart
for sailors.

Infer what spaceships find. Sketch
these horse heads and spiderwebs,
these tufted and tentacled bodies.

On watercolor paper, like fireworks,
wet drops of gold and green radiate.

A volcano in her imaginary galaxy erupts.
Lava spews bloody rocks
across a black expanse.

Now you have seen what the artist dreamed.
Now you dream. Now you see.

TAKE MY HAND...MY WHOLE LIFE

Under the moon, the moon we watched grow
from orange to snow as it climbed into black,

one of us took the hand of the other—
the whole life of the other, into her hand.

Below that full moon, through the touch
of palm skin to palm skin persisting

through the shore walk, through the lapping
or crashing of waves—although I remember

no sound—through these, the sand or the Atlantic
or maybe the spring sky computed a lunar calculus

to sync phases of once-distinct orbs with this path
from us to the horizon, this path of shine across ocean.

LETTER TO MY DAUGHTER

Dear Girl, This color I'm sending you is "cerise"
—saturated, powerful, organic—reminiscent
of you, your concentration; your mission
for meaning, for fulfillment; your sly,
deep hoots and hollers; your contradictions:
intense beyond maternal measure and at a turn,
goofy. Makes me think how your forehead
creases, "cerise," of the scar that forces
your eyebrow to hop a hairless line. You carry
this mark of boldness, reminding me always
of risk you love, and your fragility. But you mend,
did mend, we mend, and Granny will be better
soon. Saturday, maybe, they'll let her go home.
You could make her a card, one of your intricate
messages, illuminated laboriously. I marvel
at their cleverness, the fun in them, for us
who study closely—a new little face or joke
tricking around the corner. Cerise: reject
the trappings of this punk hue, allow it to meet
your rods or cones, carry it to your brain, hold it,
see it for its honesty. Sincere cerise. Serious as you.
Bold as you. True as you. Carry it beyond today.
Carry your blaze always. Long after I'm gone.
The bold mixture of you, my love. Grand
punchy cherry color you. Always, Mama

SUCCESSION

When you come home
your mother will be silent
like a queen in a new fairy tale.

In once-upon-a-time, you heard her,
her sounds the first ever to greet
your ears. You grew to her voice,
her counsel guided you.
Perhaps a vibration pings
against, or within, a secret recess,
which you will rediscover
if only everything else stills,
or if you sit quietly enough.

Her throne reminds you of succession,
of evolution, in its inevitable emptiness.

You might choose it for yourself
and picture how she dropped her shoes
to curl her stocking feet under her on the cushion.
You might take up the paperback
left on the spot, and riffle through it
hopeful for a pressed four-leafed clover,
some further evidence of resonance.

SISTERS IN DECEMBER

He disagreed about the ashes,
so his sisters set out one night
under a good December moon,
without their brother,
to the covered bridge over the Mill
and tossed the earthly bits
that had been their father
into the black water.

On the drive home, exhilarated
by the secret of the send-off,
by the rightness of the location—
(although mutable—those chips
of burnt bone, the silt
of him, has maybe ponded
on its way to the Sound,
as happens with sediment)
one sister gets scared
a guard saw them sneak
onto the bridge, illegal
after sunset, or a camera caught
this giddy made-up funeral,
also illegal, or the pale swoosh
of the sister's arm
out the small window,
returning her father
as dense gray chalk,
in an arcing slow lob,
to the brook trout
and the riverbed.

Then she is sorry to have brought up
how in the white moonbeam
the ash father glowed

through the shallow current
where the river bottom was black,
where the river margins were black,
where the coral-colored planks
of the bridge looked black,
and the surrounding sky
and trees and rocks
made one big blackness.

In daylight, next morning,
checking the view
from the covered bridge window,
she decides only other mourners
might guess about the light sand resting
on a flat boulder of basalt.
She thinks, *That's where I will be,
eventually*, some way elemental
again. On the cutbank,
stalking aquatic insects,
a green heron ignores
everything
but the flow
around its claws.

YEARNING

I do not want to be
remembered for my urine.
In this I differ from
the chow chow and Welsh corgi
who yearn to soak the earth,
to imbue the foggy air,
with their unique pee scents,
who nose through the streets in search
of smells of dogs gone by,
and recorded for canine
history until rain
rinses hydrant and trunk.
If only I could so shed
skin or salt tear as I
tread my neighborhood and thus
plant in friends' hearts my deeds,
my ways, my thinking, my art—
civil equivalent
of dogs' liquid legacy.

THOUSANDS OF EYES

Deep space archives
all happenings as light.
(Every corner mirrored, prismed.)

Traps every blush, all tossed drafts,
May's riot, yesterday's theft.

If we could travel the light-years
we'd find each action, eternal, visible—
memory of cosmos eidetic.

Waves touch us.
Waves are made by us,

this breath,
yours. The silhouette of a kiss
falls forever on a window shade.

REVERBERATIONS

Yesterday, kyanite blue
and black, a Leviathan
—at least five inches long—
flew over the rail, buzzed
and bumped and buzzed
against the balcony glass
before escaping again
while I spoke
on the phone to Aunt Bee
who had just told me
about her resident snapping turtle,
her morning's hawk sighting,
the new legs
on her pool's pollywogs.

The reverberation
of her voice in my life
since my tadpole days,
in my body's smallest bones,
amplifies our history
of love, our longing
to catalog wonders
we witness, to make
her imagination mine,
to make mine hers. Of course,
I tell her of the dragonfly,
and the dragonfly
buzzes permanently
into her own
intimate experience.

SOLSTICE CROW

for Paul Mullin

On our downward voyage through ebony hours, you love to
count seconds crossed off solar smolder, adore shouting
before stroke of solstice, hope crowds join you to note
momentousness of orbital motifs—longest or shortest,
most, most, most…Fathoming only cold gloom or
profound loss, forgetful of coming solid luminosity
—months of protracted yellow, forgetful of our
rotational rondo (or seasonally disordered),
others drown below low-color atmospheres.
Eons ago you vowed to horn-blow
upon those moments of shortest
solar showing. Now your song
jogs lost memory of cosmic
knowledge: on solstice
obscurity comes to ground.
Journeys aloft closely follow journeys down
into shadowy coal. Solar glow grows post-solstice.
Orbs bounce. Old souls drop into tombs, carom out, reborn.

OF ONE MIND

He said, We agree about everything,
how grass and pelicans, Saturn
and its satellites comprise like stuff,
of a perfect oneness.

She said, We agree about nothing,
how even gulfs and gaps, vacuums
and voids experience
gravity and pulses.

He said, We sync forever in our thinking
and will, in infinity, be *simpatico*.
I love each atom of your face
and you love mine, each month replaced.

She said, Our every step is instinct—
this breath, that gulp, those sneezes.
I love each atom of deep space,
and it loves mine—the interchange.

SUQUAMISH WATERS

a painting by Alfredo Arreguín

Above the Suquamish waters full of stars
where pelicans flap through a jeweled night

...fingered waves froth

fish   swifts   distant suns
all toss aloft
all spangly

...how right this dotted sky of scales
of green and glow
orange and crimson
where orcas dance

...every people   every thing gleams
crystalline   atomic
built of tiny other things
we cannot often see

SMOOTHIE

after Richard Brautigan

Sometimes life is a matcha smoothie.
I once read some things about matcha lattes
(which I am forever conflating
with matcha smoothies):
matcha lattes stimulate strange
feelings. Support the liver.
I want a matcha smoothie
because evening came, foggy and
cold. What a funny thing,
what I really want.

Like, talking to you.
We haven't talked for ages. It's not too late
to commit to such a pilgrimage,
at least.

If we have time left over, let's drink
matcha smoothies and, after, lie awake
(in our separate rooms) when ordinarily
we're unconscious. Experience
a contradiction of alertness.
Send dreams packing.
Sweat, as the heat seeps from our guts
into the other molecules
of us. String together dots.

That meeting in two days
calls for preparatory stillness.
Assembly of the best green powders.
Boiling, whisking, steeping.
At the reunion, I determine to sip. Sip,
with my eyes wide, wide open.

You and I warm our fingers around
matching tall mugs. I wonder if you
will burn your tongue.

WHEN WE MEET IN THE FUTURE

                What stands closest keeps us safe

  Panes   Gates   Doors   Railings

      When seen from a distance
      Lines thought to lie parallel
          Converge as they travel to the horizon

Proof   of accumulation   at
                          a
                    further point

An intersection

        WHERE WE GREET

What rides farthest from our present location
            gives us greatest perspective

    See the same thing

        from different places

            even the look
      of a clay brick
      shifts

an orbit attenuates to elliptical

Planetary objects influence the shapes of our paths

    A scaffolding   A panel   A slat
                A tile   A town

  Nowhere is sphericity irrelevant

                                      We will meet
                                      in the future

WHAT THE VIEWER UNDERSTANDS

There is no single line
to draw around any form,
yet our eyes describe all shapes
as if a heavy pencil defined each edge,
so the artist decides to collage
her self-portrait as realistically
as two dimensions allow.
When the student asks why the image,
only in places, has a sharp boundary
between figure and ground,

the artist laughs. "This is the truth
of my existence." "And why does the head,
so clear in profile of nose and mouth,
open at the back of her skull
into sky?" The artist explains,
"That is my reality." She is, after all,
made of everything inside her body
and some of the things in the space
surrounding her movements,
and, of course, the gaseous compounds
of her respiration. The class understands,

all along—this is realism,
not visual realism, state-of-being realism,
each viewer clarifying her own presence
in the world with this depiction of facts:
a strange person lives on the page
built of a daisy-filled meadow—doubtless
a few bees along with, from a photo which scissors
have sliced from *National Geographic*.
Between the woman illustrated, and her location,
its wild garden spills.

III
RIGHT PLANET

NOT A FAIRY TALE

Ask me to describe a fanciful episode in which a person
chooses to act foolishly yet her plot ends
in positive territory, and nothing comes to mind, only
serious reasons for walking out of a job or a marriage.
Can't I go somewhere silly? Shouldn't any imagining
be possible? Have I forgotten how (or been stunted)
because of vaccine headaches which hit me

yesterday as I walked homeward from Genesee Hill?
Or the tiring months of the broken bridge,
the shuttered stores, the virtual friends,
the newly dead relatives, the sad parades of coffins,
those choked, those held still to the ground,
all the grounding, all the grinding down? We need
a dose of fluff or laughter at our struggling, maybe
a story about a magic bird who delivers

a rusty key on a dirty string to a child down a dry well
who sees a slot where it fits and turns it and the wall
is really a door through which pours a delicate light
—never blinding—like the effect of sun reaching
the mossy floor of a forest through shifting spaces
between branches and leaves, the kinds of trees
where small creatures craft their twig-lichen nests

and raise broods of bright-eyed and soft-furred young,
and the child scampers into this safety to kneel
by a clean brook where, from a scooping hand,
the child drinks and drinks and drinks. Thirst slaked,
the child looks about in wonder at the solid tall trunks,
up to the tops of the alder and hemlock, and down
at the damp earth. This might be home.
This is the right planet.

This could be the place to stay.

MORSE IS WALRUS IS HOME

When away, where reddening maples line the streets,
    the telling sounds of French voices mix
        with whiffs of baguettes.

What tells of home? A dash of salt, constant raucous bellows
    from a raft of sea lions lounging on tie-downs
        in Elliott Bay?

Away, I walk Sherbrooke Street, play tourist, see old friends.
    At the museum shop, browsing books in French, I dip
        into the myth of Sedna.

The pictures depict Sedna's fingers breaking off into fish,
    her sinking into the watery below.
        The text is easy,

but I have forgotten this word, and, embarrassed, must hunt
    it on my phone. When a child, I stowed
        two words for every thing.

For reasons obscure, our teachers wanted us as fluent
    with the zoo as with terms for family,
        hues, clothing, food,

and so I know, when Away was home, I wrote *morse*
    and underneath drew a fat and tusked torpedo.
        Walrus was *morse*.

As an adult, who gets to choose, I might drop Sedna
    in favor of phrases for ordering cocktails
        never learned in school,

yet linger over the fingerless, flippered girl discovering
    herself to be a water-being,
        where *morse* tells home.

She darts between walruses, kelp, and whales, *entièrement*
    in her element, and I wonder, how many digits
        I must lose.

LIFE MEETING LIFE

Before them, briefly, an insect, winged, enormous, noisy,
    hovers in their faces,
reminds them of prehistoric dragonflies that spanned two
    feet,
recorded in Carboniferous-era coal.

The father with his daughter—or maybe it's a woman with
    her son—
stop in their rainforest walk, say, in Costa Rica, at this
    buzzing
blocking their way.

Glad for a corroborating witness, more for self-belief than
    for recounting later,
the parent's eyes meet the child's when the creature leaves
    them
in the silent moist heat.

Years after, when the child works, say, at Microsoft as a
    software engineer,
they remember the encounter as a suspension of ordinary
    clocks,
an intersection with truth. Life meeting life.

How is it she—let's just accept the parent is a mother, the
    child, a man now—
is tearless, sun heating her back, as their sweet dog, deaf
to the mail carrier, rests his unmoving head

against the iron table leg during the call to bring the animal
    doctor
who will end the sweet dog's life? Why, in the sweet dog's
last hours, isn't she lying beside him,

encircling him in her arms, wetting his fur with her crying?
    She is now.
She is now beside him on the floor.
In a text she tells her son,

We are saying goodbye at noon, and he writes back, *He is
    a good dog,*
say goodbye for me. She does. And she kisses
the soft fur head.

KNOTS

inspired by Sxwo'le *by Dan Friday*

Hundreds.

Hand-tied
and strung to hang
in this cylindrical opening.
A square scrunched
to fit the round.

A reef net to catch
glass salmon pointed against
the current.

Within the mesh of rhombuses
another circle—a hole
larger than my head—
release hatch for kings.

The artist linked
four sectors in white twine,
a bowl containing
only air.

One line, a diameter,
connects the segments.
The other two seams branch
off somewhere near the center—
but not. When fish meet
such a construct
on their anadromous journeys,
casters close the distance,

catch nourishment,
while through the knotless ring
many swimmers slip.

SOWN

after "Insipience" by Adrienne Rich

To breathe, to sleep below a safe roof
while flame danced across forests
through nights when much was done
to stem all dreams

to parry the heat and fuel
that waited for ignition
molecules of ash
invisible

to numb the aching burn
of every limb in the land

Much will be sown.
Much will be sown. Compose yourself,
measure by measure, note by note,
study the flicker of feathers
in your backyard, count starlings
allowing visits of small yellow birds
before taking their tastes
of abundance presented
this garden
this feast

LATITUDES

In northern latitudes we think we know cold dampness,
frost, and chill. It is safer to winter if honey is good
and enough. If honey be given.

We never winter without thirty pounds of honey.
We have given honey. In winter it is necessary
that honey pass through the city, a devotion of honey.

In preparing for winter we protect, in every diameter,
the spaces between dried leaves. Many words
are said for this method of wintering.

It is a guard against extremes and sudden changes—
warm, fine, a cushion. Like covering with boughs
of evergreen. Our losses arrested. Our scantlings in place.

Erasure from <u>How to Keep Bees</u> (1905)
by Anna Botsford Comstock

KNOW THE DUWAMISH WATERWAY

Do you know the Duwamish only
for its super fund-ness or for the barges

tugging, sluggish, up it to the urbane bay?
For its manhandled straightened stretch

lined with rails and warehouses, and stacked
with shipping crates? Or for the steel cranes—

equine herds of white and red—scraping
and bowing over clanging trains

that sound with terrible screams
when we would all be dreaming?

Then you do not know the Duwamish
which is all colors, which is

sky-colored, which is a dusty gray
today (but the water renders dust

such that it shines a gift of double sunrays),
the autochthonous Duwamish where osprey

hunt, where a paddler in its cold water
sees the river's tireless industry,

also its true silted banks—weedy,
and tidal, also its thin stands of alder,

its mud flats happy with Canada geese,
even a sleek dark head popping

through its surface—the resident comic, otter,
there to remind us how her great-great-grandfather

caught its stickleback or carp while swimming
alongside a cedar craft of sacred pedigree.

SURFACE EVIDENCE

On water's surface
      evidence of wind
            also identical twins
of marsh grasses upside down   a darker tinge
        also marbleized rainbow slicks
          in quiets by black mud
            also a stick
    also a white plastic bag
red words say *Thank You*

Sky rides on water's surface
        perpetuates palette
        without weight or repercussion
spreads sky gray to swamp water

stripes
   SKY
   LAND
   LAND
   SKY
      —sky lies
    also floats
below land
    on water's surface
Thank you

"EVEN BIRDS CAME DOWN"

*inspired by a photo by Robert M. L. Raynard,
titled with his caption*

even from plane trees,
even from gables,
even from nests, coops,
perches, in sadness,
not in a flock, singly,
and twisted
their small skulls
to stare cyclops-style, one eye
directed at each tragedy.

We primates
square our shoulders
for a straight gaze.
Pigeons swivel
to confront.
Isn't it fascinating,
in all their symmetry,
this avian version
of contrapposto?

ONLY FOOLS

Did we rush?

Is rush an attempt
to describe the over-fast
sensation in the chest
—bird wings, butterflies—
or the haste to consummate,
or the urgency of selves
declaring their attraction—
the zip of magnets
snapping together
with a satisfying click?

In-rushing could be
the ecstasy of mutuality.

More fools we
keeping silence when
the aim throughout humanity
ought to be a centering
on love. Oh, let's express,
now, before the cold ground
covers our lonely skeletons—
choose to be thought fools
rather than sit all alone
in our separate rooms.

BRIDGED

What if one chose to swim instead of ride,
Climbed, cold and dripping, from this blue river,
Refused towels and fires, every offer,
In preference of solitude? What if
The wet traveller had no choice—
What if an exterior force impelled
Such watery journeys? Picture it gone:
The bridge removed. The river, an ocean—
Or a widening gulf, shore receding.
Somehow, all boats turned sieve. No luxury
Of bus or bike. This is a strange country,
This of both crossings—destitute and rich,
Choosing and coercion, truth and fiction.
A land, in our minds, welcomes all drifters.

WE DO NOT ALWAYS NEED THE MAP

The train chugged into the Belgian town
too late for her touristy questions,
but with an address and a sense of direction
she set out for the hostel, dusk encroaching
like a stalker.

She remembers a step off a certain sidewalk,
which led her across the street, yes, also
off the guidebook map.

Over the next darkening minutes
she strode on, the street less trafficked,
as if a switch tripped
and everyone had gone inside.

Row houses, handsome on the last block,
loomed, alit, inexplicably sinister.
Her backpack heavier and heavier,
her armpits sweatier.

She reached the inn—spent an uneventful night.

Next day she hitchhiked with an American boy.
(His presence tricked her into uncharacteristic choices.)
They'd met over breakfast croissant
and hot chocolate.

In the limestone cavern
—the name eludes her now—
they climbed into a boat and drifted
on the River Styx
in utter invisibility.

Earlier they witnessed,
in the largest hall, Prometheus,
his torch a pinprick
in the blackness,
stealing fire for us on earth.

ON MY COUCH I AM

after Wordsworth

not a wanderer but sometimes lonely.
At times, a dancer; at times, a cloud, afloat,
aflutter—responsive to winds, soft or
strong, and the sight of yellow flowers, stars,
trees, bays, vales, all things celestial, earthly,
and inward. I see them still in this glass:
daffodils, blurry because I gaze
from so close, also crisp, because they bloom
continually in my heart, which renders
lonelinesses into solitude.

NOT KNOWING/KNOWING

Sorrowing, not knowing
whether the wife became
a widow; the son, a king,

the absence assumed a shape
which expanded as the queen
wove, then shrank daily

as she unraveled her weave,
as the characters—any one of us—
sped then slowed, our speed

wavering through gain and loss,
through surf-like flow
and ebb—a rhythm of toss

and drop, digression and growth,
our private epics lingering
then jolting forward, both,

as if a matter of fingering
for the pianist—that logic
of anatomy, instrument, and yearning

that a composer lays on paper—
a mix of outer forces and inner will,
self and what others name fate,

as if we must forever wait until
a certain boat docks,
until the hourglass sand fills

the lower globe, until clocks
stop. Did you know you might choose
when to rest, when to run, when to walk

regardless of the trickster's ruse?
Did you know you own wings?
Did you know it's up to you?

WHEN...AFTER...IN

When the thermometer reads fifteen degrees,
when the sea stretches infinitely,
when you stare unseeingly,
when you expose no sign of weakness—let alone tears,
when the smoke of your home chimneys
rises beyond the lip of your view,
you seek refuge in memory.

And at last, after weeks or eons,
after the waves jostle,
after every horizon fogs,
after you drift ashore,
after ground gains a sense of solidity,
after you stumble into company,
you zero in on one other.

In that instance,
you discover memory
matches memory.

You are returned.

HIS ODYSSEY

Recognize me when you come home.

You will have washed down the river
through ancient schists recognized
as metasediments, once silt and sand,
representatives of shorelines where surf
slapped rock, sent it crumbling
into shallow ocean, and that ocean, long gone.

While you are away, catastrophes,
various and significant to their participants,
alter us chemically. We remain recognizable.

Certain markers reveal us—
a mole at the knee, a port wine stain
on the thigh, a zinc granule in a fold of skin.

I will know you from your flight ETA,
your luggage carousel, your dusty bags…
by the fragments you carry with you of canyon,
the cells that slough off you, your scent, human, Archaean.

SUPPOSE IT IS HERE

Suppose you wake to rain.
Suppose you pack your suitcase.
Suppose your drive is long.
Suppose you sing to the radio.
Suppose the music surprises you.
Suppose you make much noise.
Suppose another driver hears you.
Suppose that human laughs.
Suppose that laughter lingers.
Suppose that recollection brings smiles.
Suppose smiles must be explained.
Suppose the telling runs nonsensical.
Suppose you hang clothes in a new closet.
Suppose you sleep between unfamiliar sheets.
Suppose you wake to thunder.
Suppose you walk out into the commotion.
Suppose the wind knocks you sideways.
Suppose you travel with the storm cell.
Suppose you forget where you are.
Suppose you begin as if the beginning can be at any location.

TUNNEL SOLO

I
Once I drove most of a tunnel's length
without seeing, behind or ahead,
any other vehicle. When driving,
one's own car is invisible; I sailed,
the white-tiled walls at my sides, the dark road
under me, leading and following.
Three minutes—or less—of time alone.
The radio snuffed at the mouth. Windowless,
also, my solitude. A sadness came.
I carried the sadness below the city
in my throat, with no desire to cry,
wanted to ingest the silence and save
the surprise of my situation, always.
I love you but am glad you stayed home.

II
You stayed home or headed to the field
while I trended north for the weekend climb
(on plastic, at the gym, not a crag
in the wilderness). So often, though, our hours
coast by, side against side on the sofa,
body next to body on the mattress
I adore for its memory, in step
on our neighborhood constitutionals,
that our friends laugh at us. "Predictable,"
they say of our near-steady proximity,
our splitting or sharing restaurant meals,
and our crossword-solving streaks. How joined
we seem to them: a single beast—a strange,
strong, happy creature with sharp teeth. We are.

III
We are joined and strong and strange and happy.
Two bodies, we may move in unison
as if wheels on an axle, our being
a machine humming, cranked, oiled, electric.
Another permutation: two bodies,
we practice individuality,
polarity, and divergence, like snails,
some animal that seldom congregates.
Both true because, of course, your thoughts and mine
stray their separate routes. I want again
a trip through the empty tunnel as if
I survived an extinction by myself.
If I shut my eyes, the black ribbon spills
before me. I see what is possible.

ONE CERTAIN THING

> *Each scenario presents a very different style of apocalypse...*
> —Katie Mack, *The End of Everything*

An end will come.
All—rendered
nonexistent.
All sentience gone—
a tenuous memory of us
under intense discussion.

How might it happen?
—a slow darkening,
our universe rent
—a densifying reversal
of The Bang energy
—an unquenchable vacuum
—a cyclic recurrence

We own a moment.

Enjoy it with me—
our immense home?
Before we go, experience
a fullness, inherent to *this*.

ABOUT THE AUTHOR

Born in Rhode Island, Pamela Hobart Carter grew up in Montreal. When she returned to the US, she graduated from high school a second time, earned two geology degrees (Bryn Mawr College and Indiana University), and became a teacher. Over more than three decades, Carter taught a variety of ages and subjects, from science pedagogy for a teaching program to art for middle school. When classrooms closed for Covid, she added make-a-poem-at-home lessons to her website: playwrightpam.wordpress.com. These days, she periodically collects poems from preschoolers via their dictation.

Carter's plays have been produced in Seattle (her home), Montreal, and Fort Worth. Her poems have been nominated for the Pushcart Prize and Best of the Net (3x). She is a 2023 Yavanika Press mixed-genre winner for *Behind the Scenes at the Eternal Everyday*, an e-chapbook of cut-ups, and a 2024 Yavanika Press mixed-genre winner for *Only Connect*, an e-chapbook of her ekphrastic poems in conversation with photographs by Londoner Robert M. L. Raynard. Some of her other publications include the poetry chapbooks *Her Imaginary Museum* (Kelsay Books) and *Held Together with Tape and Glue* (Finishing Line Press); twelve short books in easy-English for adults (written with Arleen Williams, No Talking Dogs Press); and dozens of poems and articles (in literary and teaching journals and in anthologies).

Carter is also a visual artist, gym climber, hiker, skier, and mother.